Paleo
Slow Cooker

Simple & Healthy
Gluten-Free Recipes

Large Print Edition

Amelia Simons

ISBN-13: 978-1494266004

the use or misuse of any product or information presented herein. It is the purchaser's responsibility to read and follow all instructions and warnings on all product labels.

For information, please contact the Author by email at Authors@UnitedPublishingHouse.com

Resources

Be sure to check out my other cookbooks and resources.

Complete Paleo Meals: A Paleo Cookbook Featuring Paleo Comfort Foods

Gluten-Free Slow Cooker: Easy Recipes for a Gluten Free Diet

Paleolithic Slow Cooker Soups and Stews: Healthy Family Gluten-Free Recipes

Going Paleolithic: A Quick Start Guide for a Gluten-Free Diet

4 Weeks of Fabulous Paleolithic Breakfasts

4 MORE Weeks of Fabulous Paleolithic Breakfasts

4 Weeks of Fabulous Paleolithic Lunches

4 Weeks of Fabulous Paleolithic Dinners

The Ultimate Paleolithic Collection

Table of Contents

What Exactly is Paleo Eating?

The Paleolithic way of eating includes various names like: Primal Diet, Cave Man Diet, Stone Age Diet, Hunter-Gatherer Diet, and a few others.

In a nutshell, Paleo eating is attempting to eat as our ancestors once did. It is a diet consisting of high-protein, moderate-fat foods that are not processed, modified, or tampered with. It is living a lifestyle of eating foods that are low in carbohydrates, like lean meats, vegetables, some fruits, good fats, and some starches.

Thousands of years ago, our ancestors survived, and thrived, as hunter-gathers. Their diets consisted of meat and fish, nuts and seeds, fruits and vegetables. While many years have passed, our genetic makeup has not changed much at all since then. Our ancestors were muscular, agile, quite tall, athletic, and extremely versatile. While we have enjoyed many advances in technology that have made other forms of food available to us, like grains, processed foods, and dairy, these are not as easy for our bodies to digest. Now many years later, man is often overweight, stressed, sleep deprived, lacks exercise, and dying of many diseases that experts say can often be prevented.

Apparently, a large part of our problem nowadays is agriculture! When farming became a huge part of our way of life for obtaining our food, we changed from hunter-gatherers to farmers. Consequently, man began to settle down, formed different cultures and societies, and evolved into our world today.

However, it seems as though our bodies never properly adjusted to eating the grains produced from farming. Instead of loading up on meat, vegetables and seasonal fruits, as our hunter-gatherer ancestors had to, we became a species dependent upon grains. Foods like bread, pasta, rice, and corn became a huge part of our diet.

I have read statistics that state 66% of us are overweight while 33% of us are considered obese. In addition, if this is not bad enough, it appears as though these numbers are getting worse. Clearly, something is not right and we need to do something differently.

The Paleolithic diet is an effort to go back to eating how we were biologically designed to eat. By doing so, this type of eating allows us to return to our genetic heritage and start living healthier as soon as we do. Ultimately, the foods recommended in a Paleolithic diet tend to provide our bodies with more efficient, long-lasting energy that also aids in burning fat.

Slow Cooking Paleolithic Style

One of the things I have enjoyed doing is experimenting with making Paleo recipes in my slow cooker. As a busy wife and mother, I often have things I would rather do (and often have to do) than spend a lot of time in the kitchen.

Having accumulated several different slow cookers in various sizes, it has been fun to create dips, side dishes and entrees in my slow cookers. I even challenge myself sometimes to see how many slow cookers I can have going all at the same time! While I have fun doing this some days, most all the recipes included in this book will use a single 6-quart sized slow cooker.

In this cookbook, my recipes focus on being Paleolithic friendly while offering the simplicity and ease of cleanup when cooking in a slow cooker.

I want to point out a few things about this cookbook as you begin your journey:

1. This cookbook, just like all my other ones, is Paleo friendly. I've created my recipes without grains, which eliminates a lot of gluten issues. Be sure to read labels and become familiar with ingredients that may contain gluten. (That's a science project all it's own!)

2. I'm not quite as strict about my Paleolithic lifestyle as some are. However, like many other Paleolithic eaters I've read about and follow online, I enjoy a few selective dairy products.

Just as I've done for a few decades, I use butter occasionally in my cooking, although now it is always grass-fed butter. For those who have problems with dairy and want to enjoy the flavor of butter, clarified butter or ghee work great because the milk solids are removed.

To be honest, there is just no way I am going to give up my Half-and-Half in my coffee – at least not as of this writing. Many in the Paleo community choose not to eat dairy, however, many do. I happen to enjoy dairy and do not experience any negative side effects. So, occasionally you will see a dairy product mentioned, but it is **always optional**. Feel free to eliminate it if you desire, or have to because of intolerance, or substitute it with an ingredient you like instead.

If you can tolerate cheese and you want to use some (like in Sweet Lasagna (p. 108), make sure you buy **aged** cheeses. As cheese ages, it loses lactose (milk sugar), so the older it is, the better tolerated it is.

3. Buy organic, pasture-fed, grass-fed, range free, hormone free, nitrite/nitrate-free, sugar free, gluten free, wild, and as many unprocessed foods as your budget will allow. I know money is tight when it comes to buying grass-fed/pasture-fed beef, pork, and poultry.

Many are not able to buy higher-price ingredients so the ingredients listed in each recipe for the most part are "generic" ingredients.

Strive to buy the leanest and nicest cuts of meat you can afford. While you are learning to cook Paleolithic-style, focus on the foods allowed and how to use them in combination – all while hoping for the day when you'll notice the money you've been saving on "junk food" will allow you to afford the nicer and better cuts of meats and other Paleo foods.

Any place that you see "GF" it stands for "gluten free."

4. Occasionally, there will be a recipe that has a little raw honey or pure maple syrup included in it. Once again, feel free to eliminate it or include it – it's up to you. This one ingredient will not change the texture or affect the flavor of the recipe much at all if you choose to leave it out or include it.

5. I have included a few homemade recipes for ingredients like Worcestershire sauce (p. 17) and BBQ sauce (p. 47). It is difficult to find sauces that do not include soy and sugars.

6. Making your own broths allows you to know exactly what is in them. However, if you do not have time or do not desire to, there is a brand called "More Than Gourmet®" that is excellent and at this writing is considered to be 100% Paleolithic. If you cannot find them in your grocery store, be sure to check online.

Slow Cooker Tips

To help you with the techniques and recipes contained in this cookbook, I thought it might be helpful to offer you a few tips on what to look for when buying a slow cooker and some general rules that apply to cooking with one.

Most all the recipes in this cookbook use a 6-quart slow cooker. There are smaller ones you can purchase to allow you to cook side dishes or beverages while you are cooking your main entrée in the 6-quart slow cooker. Slow cooking is fun, saves you money on your electric bill, dinner preparations are simplified, and cleanup is fast.

When you go looking to purchase a slow cooker, be sure to look for one that has a removable liner. This makes them much easier to clean. Having had ones that do not, I cannot stress how important this tip really is! However, if you already own one that does not have a removable liner, you can line your slow cooker with a cooking bag so that you will not have any cleanup.

For most slow cookers, the LOW setting is meant to reach about 200 degrees F while the HIGH setting will reach 300 degrees F. Because the minimum safe temperature for cooking food is 140 degrees F, this makes slow cooking a safe alternative to oven cooking. (Be sure to check the temperature of the food you are cooking sometime to make sure your slow cooker meets these standards.)

Experts advise that you bring the temperature of the food you are cooking up to 140 degrees F as quickly as possible. Consequently, be advised that you should not put food that is frozen into your slow cooker. Defrost most cuts of meats and other dense food items before you place them into the slow cooker.

As a rule, two hours of cooking on LOW is equivalent to cooking one hour on HIGH.

Do your best NOT to overload your slow cooker. Try not to fill it more than two-thirds of the way full to allow proper cooking of the contents.

When cooking large cuts of meat, allow about 8 hours of cooking time if cooking on the low setting.

Slow cooking can be very economical because you can use cheaper cuts of meat, yet these come out moist and tender after being cooked this way.

Once your slow cooker is heated, try not to lift the lid because it releases a lot of the heat that is built up. It takes approximately 20 extra minutes for the slow cooker to regain the temperature it was before you lifted the lid.

Wait to add your spices until the last hour. If you put them in at the beginning, they will lose their punch and flavor.

One of the things I learned when adapting recipes for the slow cooker was to cut any liquids called for by one-third to one-half of what is called for. Liquids do not cook out and disappear as they do on the stovetop so try cutting back on them at the start. The only exception to this would be if you are making a soup in your slow cooker.

Depending upon what you cooked in your slow cooker, they are quite easy to clean. They just take a few minutes of tender-loving care. Fill the liner with hot soapy water, or submerge it into a sink of hot soapy water. If food is stuck on, allow it to sit for 15 to 20 minutes, and then use a sponge or netted cleaning pad to loosen the baked-on food. Do not use harsh abrasive cleaners or metal scratchy pads.

It is best to remove fats from cuts of meat and poultry before you cook them.

Something I learned that might surprise you as it did me is that carrots and onions should be placed on the **bottom** of the slow cooker, under the meat. Apparently, the meat cooks faster than these types of vegetables so you want them on the bottom where the heat is higher.

Most slow cooker liners that can be removed may be used safely in ovens up to 400 degrees F.

Almost all slow cooker liners are capable of being placed in the microwave with the lid removed.

Slow cookers preserve a lot of the minerals and vitamins in your vegetables than conventional cooking

On average, most dishes are cheaper to cook in your slow cooker than they would be if you had to use your oven. Sometimes items cooked on the stovetop are a toss up.

Finally, there are just some things you can't beat when using a slow cooker to make your meals – no matter what it costs to use them:

It makes tougher cuts of meat tender

You can prepare dinner in the morning, leaving you free to do other things throughout the day

The smells during the day are amazing!

You can take a nap and wake up to dinner fully cooked – my favorite!

Beef

Dishes

Heavenly Short Ribs

I cannot think of a better way to get your house smelling great and to get your crew excited about dinnertime than with this delicious dish. It even tastes better than it smells!

Ingredients:

- 2 tablespoons coconut oil
- 5 pounds beef short ribs
- 2 teaspoons kosher salt
- 1 teaspoon black pepper
- 1 large onion, chopped
- 1½ cups chicken broth
- 2 cups apple cider vinegar
- ⅔ cup raw honey (optional)
- 2 teaspoons Frank's hot sauce
- 14 ounces tomato paste
- 1½ cups beef broth
- ½ cup Paleolithic-style Worcestershire sauce (see below for homemade recipe)
- ½ cup coconut aminos

- 2 teaspoons chili powder
- 5 cloves of garlic, minced

Directions:

1. Heat a large frying pan on the stovetop with the coconut oil

2. Rub the salt and pepper into the ribs

3. Place the seasoned ribs into the frying pan and brown them on both sides

4. Turn on your slow cooker to HIGH to get it warmed up

5. Transfer the ribs into your slow cooker

6. Combine the remaining ingredients together in a medium bowl and mix thoroughly

7. Now pour the mixture over the ribs

8. Place the lid onto the slow cooker and cook on HIGH for 2 hours, then lower the temperature to LOW for 4 hours, OR you can cook them on LOW for 8 hours.

Makes 6 servings (with possible leftovers)

~ ~ ~ ~ ~ ~ ~ ~

Homemade Worcestershire Sauce:

Here is a Paleolithic condiment you can make yourself and keep on hand whenever you find a recipe you want to convert to Paleolithic.

- 1 cup apple cider vinegar
- ¼ cup coconut aminos
- ¼ cup Thai fish sauce (optional, but makes it taste great)
- ¼ cup water
- ¼ teaspoon coarse black pepper
- ½ teaspoon dry mustard
- ½ teaspoon onion powder
- ¼ teaspoon ground cinnamon
- ½ teaspoon ground ginger
- ½ teaspoon garlic powder

Directions:

1. Place all the ingredients into a saucepan on your stovetop

2. Bring to a boil and allow it to simmer for 1 to 2 minutes

3. Cool and store in a container in your refrigerator

Pot Roast with Turnips

It has been a slight challenge to find vegetables to substitute for white potatoes with a roast. Thankfully, there is the turnip! When cooked with a roast, it is a great substitute. Parsnips are a good substitute as well so feel free to use either one in this recipe and in ones you already enjoy. Close your eyes and you might not even know the difference.

Ingredients:

- 2 tablespoons coconut oil
- 5 - 6 pound bottom round or chuck roast
- 5 cloves garlic, minced
- 2 onions, diced
- 2 teaspoons oregano
- 1 teaspoon kosher or sea salt
- 1 teaspoon black pepper
- 4 medium carrots, peeled and sliced into bite-sized pieces
- 3 celery stalks, chopped into bite-sized pieces

- 4 turnips or parsnips, peeled and chopped into bite size pieces
- 1 cup beef broth
- 1 cup red wine vinegar

Directions:

1. Turn your slow cooker on HIGH while you begin to prepare your dish

2. In a large skillet, heat up the coconut oil

3. Once the oil is hot, place the roast into the pan and sear it on all sides – about 2 minutes each side

4. Transfer the roast to the slow cooker

5. Place all the remaining ingredients into the cooker and place the lid on

6. Leave the cooker on HIGH for two hours, then turn down to LOW for 5 to 6 more hours. Otherwise, cook on LOW for 8 to 9 hours.

Makes 6 – 8 servings

Beef Stew

This recipe is always a favorite recipe for me to make when it starts to get cold outside. Not only is it flavorful, but by using some arrowroot, you get some gravy at the end, too!

Ingredients:

- 2 tablespoons coconut oil OR 6 slices of nitrite/nitrate free bacon cut into pieces
- 4 pounds stew meat
- 3 large carrots, peeled and cut into chunks
- 1 large onion, chopped
- 8 ounces sliced mushrooms
- 3 cloves garlic, minced
- 1 cup beef broth
- 1 cup red wine vinegar
- 1 teaspoon dried marjoram
- 1½ tablespoons homemade Worcestershire sauce (p. 15)
- 2 teaspoons salt
- 1 teaspoon pepper

- 1½ tablespoons arrowroot powder

Directions:

1. Turn your slow cooker on HIGH as you prepare the meat on the stovetop

2. In a large skillet, heat up the coconut oil OR cook the bacon pieces then drain on paper towel

3. Add the stew meat and brown the pieces on all sides in the coconut oil OR with some of the bacon grease

4. Transfer the meat pieces and the drippings in the skillet into the slow cooker

5. Add all the remaining ingredients to the slow cooker EXCEPT the coconut flour

6. Leave the temperature setting on HIGH and cook for 5 hours OR place the slow cooker on LOW and cook for 8 hours

7. A few minutes before serving, mix the arrowroot powder with a small amount of cold water to make a paste

8. Stir into the slow cooker to thicken the juices. Add more if needed

9. Serve over mashed cauliflower if desired

Makes 6 servings

Brewed & Stewed Beef

Coffee certainly seems like an unlikely ingredient in this pot roast, but hey, it is good! Try it if coffee is one of your favorite beverages like it is for me. And even if it isn't, it might be after you make this dish.

Ingredients:

- 2 tablespoons coconut oil
- 7 – 8 pound sirloin tip or chuck roast
- 2 large onions, sliced
- 8 garlic cloves, minced
- 2 tablespoons balsamic vinegar
- ½ cup coffee
- 2 teaspoons kosher or sea salt
- 1 teaspoon black pepper
- 1 teaspoon marjoram

Directions:

1. Place a large skillet on your stovetop and heat up the coconut oil

2. Put the roast into the skillet and brown on all sides

3. While the meat is browning, turn your slow cooker on HIGH

4. Place the onion slices and minced garlic on the bottom of your cooker

5. When meat is browned, place the roast on top of the garlic and onions in the cooker

6. Pour the vinegar and coffee over the meat

7. Sprinkle the salt, pepper, and marjoram over the meat

8. Put your cooker on LOW and cook for 9 to 10 hours

Serves 8

Oriental Pepper Steak

This dish will have you thinking you have just purchased an entrée from a Chinese restaurant. Since the Paleolithic lifestyle does not include regular rice, you can enjoy this dish over spaghetti squash if you wish.

Ingredients:

- 3 pounds round or sirloin steak
- 2 tablespoons coconut oil
- 1 tablespoon coarse black pepper
- 2 teaspoons kosher or sea salt
- ¼ cup coconut aminos
- 2 cloves of garlic, minced
- 16 ounces water chestnuts, drained
- 1 large onion, sliced, then separated into rings
- 1 large green pepper, sliced into strips
- 16 ounces diced tomatoes
- 16 ounces broccoli sprouts, rinsed and drained

Directions:

1. Turn your slow cooker on HIGH and allow it to heat up

2. Using a cutting board and sharp knife, cut across the grain of the meat, making thin strips of the steak

3. On the stovetop, heat up the coconut oil, then place the meat strips in it and brown them

4. Place the browned meat into the bottom of the slow cooker

5. Mix the salt and pepper together in a bowl, then sprinkle it on to the meat

6. Sprinkle the coconut aminos then the garlic over the top of the meat

7. Now gently put in the water chestnuts, onion rings, pepper strips and diced tomatoes

8. Place the lid on the slow cooker and cook on LOW for 6 to 7 hours

9. One hour before servings, put in the sprouts to allow them to heat up

Serves 6

Chicken
Dishes

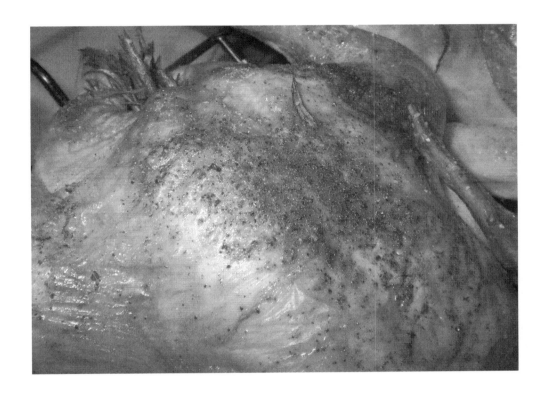

Chicken Cacciatore

This recipe is not hard to make at all. Basically, you put everything into the slow cooker, turn it on, then come back hours later and eat! My favorite is to put this over spaghetti squash.

Ingredients:

- 3 tablespoons coconut oil, melted
- 2 pounds chicken breast
- 2 stalks of celery, sliced
- 4 garlic cloves, minced
- 1 large onion, chopped
- 3 large bell peppers – any color
- 15 ounces diced tomatoes
- 1 tablespoon oregano

Directions:

1. Turn your slow cooker on HIGH while you get your ingredients ready

2. Place the coconut oil in the bottom and allow it to melt

3. Place the remaining ingredients into the slow cooker and reduce the slow cooker to LOW

4. Cook for 7 to 8 hours

5. Serve over spaghetti squash if desired

Makes 4 to 6 servings

Chicken Fajitas

I really enjoy Mexican food and these chicken fajitas are really good. While regular tortillas are not Paleolithic, there are coconut flour tortillas recipes online, or just put it on a big romaine lettuce leaf as I do. I also like this mixture over spaghetti squash.

- 2 tablespoons coconut oil
- 2 large onion, sliced and popped into rings
- 4 bell peppers, sliced into rings
- 3 pounds boneless chicken breasts
- ¾ cup chicken broth
- 2 tablespoons lime juice
- 2 tablespoons cumin
- 1 teaspoon salt
- 2 tablespoons chili powder

Directions:

1. Turn your slow cooker up to HIGH to get it warmed up
2. Place the coconut oil in the bottom of the slow cooker

3. Put the onion rings and pepper rings on the bottom

4. Place the chicken breast pieces in next

5. Pour in the chicken broth and lime juice

6. Mix the cumin, salt, and chili powder together in a small bowl

7. Now sprinkle seasonings over the chicken

8. Place the lid on the cooker and cook on HIGH for 4 to 5 hours or turn it down to LOW and cook for 8 hours

9. When finished, serve with your favorite fajita fixings over spaghetti squash or on large romaine lettuce leaves

Makes 6 to 8 servings

Stuffed Peppers with Chicken

These stuffed peppers are delicious and have a Mexican twist to them. While there are a lot of seasonings in this recipe, trust me – it's worth the effort.

You will need a slow cooker that has a removable liner because we are going to finish cooking these babies in the oven. (This makes about 6 to 8 servings.)

Ingredients:

- 4 large boneless chicken breasts
- 4 ounce can diced jalapenos
- 10 ounce can Ro-tel diced tomatoes
- 1 small onion, chopped
- ½ cup chicken broth
- ¾ teaspoon garlic powder
- ½ teaspoon cayenne pepper
- ¼ teaspoon oregano
- 1 teaspoon crushed red peppers
- 1 teaspoon salt
- 1 teaspoon cumin
- 2 teaspoons onion powder

- 4 – 5 large bell peppers, depending upon the amount of filling
- 2 cups of your favorite salsa
- Shredded aged cheese for topping (optional, if you are okay with eating dairy)

Directions:

1. Turn your slow cooker on HIGH as you get your ingredients together

2. Place the chicken breasts into the bottom of the slow cooker

3. Put all the ingredients in on top of the chicken pieces (down through the onion powder)

4. Turn the cooker down to LOW and cook for 6 to 7 hours

5. Preheat your oven to 350 degrees

6. Shred the chicken using two forks and mix up the ingredients well that are inside the slow cooker

7. Take your bell peppers and cut off the top of the peppers and clean out the seeds inside

8. Rinse under water to help remove any remaining seeds

9. Mix in the salsa with the chicken mixture and stir together

10. Stuff the peppers with the chicken and set each one aside as you fill it

11. Return the peppers to the slow cooker liner, allowing the peppers to lean against each other for support

12. Cover the tops of the peppers with a little more salsa and shredded cheese if desired

13. Place in your preheated oven and bake until the peppers are soft – approximately 25 to 30 minutes

Chicken Italiano

This recipe is so easy to make and gets me excited about dinnertime because it smells so good while it's cooking. This dish is delicious served over spaghetti squash, like a cacciatore or just plain.

Ingredients:

- 2 tablespoons coconut oil
- 3 pounds skinless chicken breast meat or thighs, cut into strips
- 2 carrots, peeled and sliced
- 2 onions, sliced and popped into rings
- 2 zucchini, peeled and sliced or cubed
- 3 cans of 14.5 ounces of tomatoes with Italian herbs
- ½ can tomato paste
- 4 garlic cloves, minced
- 1 teaspoon red pepper flakes
- 2 teaspoons raw honey (optional)

Directions:

1. Turn your slow cooker on HIGH while getting your ingredients ready

2. Put your coconut oil in the bottom of the slow cooker

3. Place the chicken strips, carrots, onions, and zucchini into the cooker

4. In a bowl, combine the tomatoes, tomato paste, garlic, pepper flakes, and honey and mix together

5. Pour over the chicken and vegetables

6. Turn slow cooker down to LOW and cook for 8 to 9 hours

Makes 6 servings

Layered Chicken Salad

You will really like the way this dish looks, especially if you layer it in a glass dish with tall sides. It is great to take to a potluck dinner at a friend's house or to serve something delicious and pretty to your family.

Ingredients:

- 3 pounds boneless skinless chicken breasts
- 1½ teaspoons cumin
- 2 teaspoons kosher or sea salt
- 1 teaspoon black pepper
- 1½ teaspoons garlic powder
- 1 teaspoon cayenne pepper
- 2 onions, chopped
- 1 cup salsa verde (Trader Joe's is good)
- 1 head of romaine lettuce, shredded
- 2 avocados, peeled and sliced
- ½ cup black olives, sliced
- 1 cup chopped fresh tomatoes
- Additional salsa verde from a jar for topping (optional)

Directions:

1. Turn your slow cooker on HIGH while you get your ingredients ready

2. Place the chicken breast on the bottom of the slow cooker

3. Sprinkle on the cumin, salt, pepper, garlic, and cayenne

4. Now sprinkle the onion pieces on top of the spices

5. Pour the salsa on top

6. Turn the slow cooker down to LOW and cook for 7 hours

7. When the time comes, take two big forks and shred the chicken

8. Mix the ingredients in the slow cooker thoroughly

9. Remove the chicken, place it in a shallow bowl and allow it to cool for about 20 minutes

10. Now take the shredded lettuce and place it in the bottom of the serving dish

11. Top it with the shredded chicken, followed by the avocado slices, black olives, fresh tomatoes, and salsa verde

Makes 6 to 8 servings

Pork
Dishes

BBQ Baby Back Ribs

I really like great tasting ribs and these definitely qualify. They fall off the bone and depending upon the BBQ sauce you use, they can be sweet or spicy. Whatever you choose, they are just downright yummy!

Ingredients

- 2 tablespoons coarse black pepper
- 3 tablespoons kosher or sea salt
- 4 tablespoons paprika
- 2 teaspoons cayenne powder
- 1 tablespoon crushed red pepper
- 2 tablespoons garlic powder
- 2 tablespoons onion powder
- 2 racks of baby back pork ribs (they will be stacked on each other in your slow cooker)
- 2 teaspoons coconut oil
- Your favorite GF and sugar-free BBQ sauce (or make your own homemade BBQ sauce below)

Directions:

1. Turn your slow cooker on LOW while you get your ingredients ready

2. Mix the pepper, salt, paprika, cayenne, red pepper, garlic, and onion powder together in a small bowl

3. Place the rib rack out on a big cookie sheet

4. Rub the spices into the meaty side of the rack

5. Allow the rack to reach room temperature – about 45 minutes to one hour

6. Place the coconut oil in the bottom of the slow cooker

7. Cut the rack into serving-sized pieces and place inside the slow cooker. Don't worry if they overlap each other

8. Cook on LOW for 7 hours, rotating the ribs halfway through

9. After 7 hours, take your BBQ sauce and brush it on to the ribs as best you can

10. Cover and turn slow cooker to HIGH for one hour

Makes 4 servings

Homemade BBQ sauce

It can be difficult to find a barbecue sauce that is sugar free and free of some additives that are not Paleolithic-friendly. Try this one. I know you will like it! We certainly do at our house.

- 1½ cups beef broth
- 1 small (6 ounce) can tomato paste
- 1/8 cup spicy mustard
- 4 teaspoons coconut oil
- 1/8 cup apple cider vinegar
- ¼ cup coconut aminos
- 4 garlic cloves, minced
- 1 small onions, chopped
- ¾ teaspoon paprika
- 2 tablespoons chili powder
- ½ teaspoon red pepper flakes
- 1½ teaspoons sea salt

1. Place all the ingredients into a medium saucepan with a lid over medium to low heat. You want to

make sure your fire isn't too hot so the tomato paste doesn't burn

2. Cover and simmer for one hour

3. Using an immersion blender, carefully blend the ingredients so the sauce is nice and smooth

4. Cool then keep in the refrigerator

Very Berry Good Pork Roast

This pork roast is amazing! The spices along with the fruit make this a treat at our house.

Ingredients:

- 4 – 5 pound pork roast
- 2 teaspoons kosher or sea salt
- 2 teaspoons coarse black pepper
- 1 tablespoon ground cinnamon
- 1 tablespoon ground nutmeg
- 2 teaspoons ground cloves
- 2 teaspoons orange peel or zest from two oranges
- 1/3 cup pure maple syrup – grade B (optional)
- 2 pounds frozen mixed berries or just cherries

Directions:

1. Turn your slow cooker on to HIGH while you get your ingredients ready

2. Place the pork roast in the bottom of the slow cooker and season it with the salt and pepper

3. Combine the cinnamon, nutmeg, cloves, orange zest, and maple syrup and mix together

4. Pour over the meat

5. Pour the frozen berries over the meat and place the lid on top of the slow cooker

6. Cook on LOW for 10 hours

7. If you wish, you can shred the meat and stir it in with the fruit and sauce before serving

Makes 8 to 10 servings

Simply Peachy Pork Roast

This pork roast is so easy to prepare but the results you get will taste like you slaved in the kitchen. Take your pick of using peach preserves or apricot. Either way, the results are sensational.

Ingredients:

- 4 pound pork loin
- 12 ounces **unsweetened** peach or apricot preserves
- 1 cup chicken broth
- ¼ cup cold water
- 1 tablespoon arrowroot powder

Directions:

1. Turn your slow cooker on HIGH as you begin to get your ingredients ready

2. Place the pork loin in the bottom of the slow cooker

3. Now pour the chicken broth over the pork

4. Spoon the preserves over the pork

5. Place the lid on the cooker and lower the temperature to LOW

6. Cook for 7 hours or until tender

7. If you desire a gravy with your pork, do the following after you remove the pork from the slow cooker:

8. Mix the arrowroot powder in with the water, forming a paste

9. Pour the paste into the liquid in the slow cooker and stir until thickened. (If necessary, heat on top of the stove in a saucepan).

Makes 6 to 8 servings

Fruit & Nutty Pork Chops

I really enjoy fruit and nuts so whenever I can enjoy them as a main dish, I am all over it. This dish is delightful and is one we enjoy eating along with steamed broccoli. Hope it becomes a family favorite at your house, too.

Ingredients:

- 2 tablespoons coconut oil
- 5 - 6 thick-sliced pork chops or 8 to 10 regularly sliced ones
- 2 tart apples, peeled and cut into slices
- 1 cup walnuts, coarsely chopped
- 2 small onions or 1 large onion, chopped
- 2 cloves of garlic, minced
- 1 tablespoon kosher or sea salt
- 2 teaspoons coarse black pepper
- 2 teaspoons cinnamon
- 1 tablespoon raw honey or pure maple syrup (optional)

Directions:

1. Turn your slow cooker on HIGH so it can warm up

2. Place a large frying pan on the stovetop with the coconut oil in it

3. Once the oil is hot, brown the pork chops on each side for about 2 to 3 minutes on each side

4. Now place the pork chops into the slow cooker

5. Place the apple slices into the frying pan, along with the walnuts, onions, garlic, salt, and pepper and cook until onions and apples are softened

6. Pour this mixture over the pork chops

7. Sprinkle the cinnamon over the meat and drizzle the honey over the meat

8. Cover and lower the temperature to LOW and cook for 8 hours OR you can set the temperature on HIGH for 2 hours, then LOW for 4 hours

Makes 6 to 8 servings

Johnny's Pork Roast

Apples and pork make a lovely match and this dish is no exception. It is extremely easy to prepare and fills the house with beautiful smells of a meal greatly anticipated. Do not let the "easy" part fool you.

Ingredients:

- 2 tablespoons coconut oil
- 4 pound pork loin
- 2 teaspoons kosher or sea salt
- 2 teaspoons coarse black pepper
- 5 apples, peeled, cored, and cut into slices
- ½ cup unsweetened apple juice
- 2 tablespoons raw honey or pure maple syrup (optional)
- 1½ teaspoons ground ginger

Directions:

1. Turn your slow cooker on HIGH while you get your ingredients ready

2. In a large saucepan, place the coconut oil and allow it to heat

3. Place the pork loin in the saucepan and brown on all sides

4. Transfer the pork to your slow cooker

5. Sprinkle the meat with the salt and pepper

6. Now put in the apple slices in the slow cooker around the meat

7. In a measuring cup, stir together the apple juice and raw honey and ground ginger (Heat for a minute to liquefy the honey to make stirring easier if necessary)

8. Pour the apple mixture over the pork

9. Place the lid on the cooker and turn the temperature down to LOW

10. Cook for 10 hours on LOW or 6 to 7 on HIGH

Makes 6 to 8 servings

Lamb

Dishes

Slow Curried Lamb

This is truly a delicious dish. It is almost like a lamb stew. And served over spaghetti squash, you have a scrumptious dish to warm you from the inside out.

Ingredients:

- 2 tablespoons coconut oil
- 3 pounds lamb shoulder or stew meat, cut into cubes
- 2 garlic cloves, minced
- 2 onions, chopped
- 2 cups diced carrots
- 1½ teaspoons kosher or sea salt
- 1 teaspoon coarse black pepper
- ¼ teaspoon coriander
- ¼ teaspoon cumin
- ¼ teaspoon cinnamon
- ¼ teaspoon cayenne pepper
- 1½ tablespoons curry powder
- Juice from 2 lemons
- 1 cup unsweetened pineapple juice
- 2 tablespoons tomato paste

- 3 apples, peeled, cored, and chopped
- 1½ tablespoons arrowroot powder
- Enough cold water to make a thin paste with arrowroot powder

Directions:

1. Turn your slow cooker on HIGH as you prepare your ingredients

2. On your stovetop, place the coconut oil and heat it up

3. Add the lamb cubes and brown them on all sides

4. Transfer the lamb cubes to your slow cooker

5. In the same saucepan, sauté the garlic and onions until tender

6. Place the garlic and onions into the slow cooker with the lamb

7. To the lamb add the carrots, salt, pepper, coriander, cumin, cinnamon, cayenne pepper, and curry

8. In a separate bowl, mix the lemon juice, pineapple juice, and tomato paste

9. Pour the juice over the lamb

10. Now add the chopped apples

11. Cover the cooker with the lid and cook on HIGH for 4 to 5 hours or on LOW for 8 to 9 hours

12. Before ready to serve, mix the ingredients gently in the slow cooker

13. In a separate cup, add the arrowroot powder and slowly add cold water and mix to create a thin paste

14. Stir the arrowroot paste into the lamb to thicken

15. Delicious!

Makes 6-8 servings

Slow Cooker Lamb Chops

This makes a delightful and flavorful recipe and is easy to make. While many people think of having lamb more in the fall, if you like it, then any time of year is perfect.

Ingredients:

- 2 tablespoons coconut oil
- 4 tablespoons coconut flour
- 8 lamb loin chops
- ⅔ cup beef broth or chicken broth
- 14.5 ounce can diced tomatoes
- 2 cloves of garlic, minced
- 2 tablespoons tomato paste
- 4 celery stalks, sliced
- 2 teaspoons kosher or sea salt
- 1 teaspoon coarse black pepper
- 1 teaspoon crushed red peppers (for a little heat)
- ½ teaspoon dried thyme
- 1 teaspoon dried oregano

Directions:

1. Turn your slow cooker on HIGH while you prepare your dish

2. On the stovetop, place the coconut oil in a large frying pan and heat

3. Coat the lamb chops with the coconut flour then place in the frying pan with the hot oil

4. Brown quickly, then transfer the chops to the slow cooker

5. In a separate bowl, combine the remaining ingredients and mix thoroughly

6. Pour the mixture over the lamb chops

7. Place the lid on the slow cooker and cook on HIGH for 1 hour

8. Turn the slow cooker down to LOW and cook for 6 to 7 hours

Makes 4 to 6 servings

Sweet Potatoes & Curried Lamb

This dish is a real crowd pleaser at our house. It smells good when it is cooking and when served over mashed cauliflower rice, you have got yourself a winner every time.

Ingredients:

- 2 tablespoons coconut oil
- 3 pounds lamb stew meat
- 2 onions, chopped
- 3 cloves of garlic, minced
- 3 large sweet potato, peeled and diced
- 1 tablespoon ground cumin
- 2 teaspoons curry powder
- 1 tablespoon ground coriander
- 1 tablespoon ground turmeric
- 4 cups chicken stock
- 4 cups fresh spinach
- ⅔ cup coconut milk

Directions:

1. Turn your slow cooker on to HIGH as you prepare your ingredients

2. Place a frying pan on your stovetop with the coconut oil and heat

3. Brown the lamb pieces and then place them into the slow cooker

4. Add the onion and garlic to the frying pan and sauté until tender

5. Add the onion and garlic to the slow cooker

6. Place the sweet potato dices to the slow cooker

7. Sprinkle the spices on top of the lamb

8. Pour in the chicken stock

9. Turn the temperature of the slow cooker down to LOW and cook for 6 to 7 hours

10. One hour before serving, add the fresh spinach and the coconut milk to the slow cooker

Makes 4 to 6 servings

Lamb Stew with Vegetables

This stew is very tasty with garlic, bay leaves, and oregano, making it a great meal for warm weather. Serve it over spaghetti squash and it just might become a tradition.

Ingredients:

- 3 tablespoons coconut oil
- 3 pounds boneless leg of lamb, trimmed and cut into large diced pieces
- Salt and pepper to season lamb pieces while browning
- 3 large onions, thinly sliced
- 5 cloves garlic, minced
- 2 (14-ounce) cans diced tomatoes, undrained
- 1 teaspoon dried oregano
- 2 large parsnips, peeled and cut into dices
- 1 pound green beans cut into small pieces
- 2 eggplants, peeled and cut into dices
- 2 zucchini, peeled and cut into dices
- 6 bay leaves
- 3 tablespoons chopped fresh parsley

Directions:

1. Turn your slow cooker on to HIGH while you prepare your ingredients

2. Place a large frying pan on your stovetop and put the coconut oil in to heat up

3. Once the oil is hot, place the lamb pieces into the frying pan and lightly season the lamb with salt and pepper

4. Once the lamb is well browned, transfer the meat to the slow cooker

5. Add the onions and garlic to the frying pan and sauté until tender

6. Now add the cans of tomatoes and oregano to the onions and garlic and heat to a gentle boil

7. Spoon half the tomato mixture over the lamb in the slow cooker

8. Now add the parsnips and lightly season with salt and pepper

9. Add the green beans and season with salt and pepper

10. Place the eggplant on as the next layer and lightly season with salt and pepper

11. Place the zucchini dices in last and season with salt and pepper

12. Pour the remaining tomato mixture over the vegetables

13. Top with the bay leaves

14. Place the cover on the slow cooker and either leave the cooker on HIGH for 4 to 5 hours, or turn it down to LOW and cook for 8 to 9 hours

15. Remove the bay leaves before serving

Makes 8 to 10 servings

Seafood &

Fish Dishes

Pokey Seafood Gumbo

I grew up around the water and have fond memories of catching crab and shrimp right out of the water. My grandfather ran a restaurant so we always had some good eats growing up. I think you will like this gumbo. It does bring back some wonderful memories.

Ingredients:

- 2 tablespoons coconut oil
- 3 garlic cloves, minced
- 2 medium onions, chopped
- 2 celery stalks, sliced
- 2 bell peppers, seeded and chopped
- 14 ounce can of diced tomatoes, undrained
- 2 cups chicken broth
- 2 tablespoons Cajun seasoning
- 2 tablespoons homemade Worcestershire sauce (p. 15)
- 2 teaspoons kosher or sea salt
- 1 teaspoon dried thyme leaves
- 2 bay leaves
- 1½ pounds raw shrimp, thawed

- 1½ pounds fresh or frozen crabmeat, thawed
- 10 ounce bag frozen sliced okra, thawed

Directions:

1. Turn your slow cooker on HIGH so it can warm up while you get your ingredients ready

2. In a large frying pan on the stove, heat up the coconut oil

3. Sauté the garlic, onions, celery and bell peppers until tender

4. Transfer the cooked vegetables to your slow cooker

5. Pour the diced tomatoes and the chicken broth into the slow cooker

6. Add the Cajun seasoning, Worcestershire sauce, salt, thyme, and bay leaves

7. Place the lid on the slow cooker and turn the temperature down to LOW

8. Cook on LOW for 4 hours

9. Add the shrimp, crabmeat, and okra to the cooker and cook for 1 hour longer

Makes 6 to 8 servings

Shrimp Marinara

Marinara sauces are always yummy and smell so good while they are cooking. Shrimp in this one gives it a slight twist but still tastes great over spaghetti squash.

Ingredients:

- 2 (14.5 ounce) cans of diced tomatoes, undrained
- 2 (6-ounce) cans tomato paste
- 4 tablespoons fresh parsley, chopped
- 2 onions, chopped
- 2 garlic cloves, minced
- 2 teaspoons kosher or sea salt
- 1 teaspoon coarse black pepper
- 1 teaspoon dried basil
- 2 teaspoons dried oregano
- 2 pounds cooked shrimp

Directions:

1. Turn your slow cooker on HIGH while you get your ingredients ready

2. Pour the diced tomatoes into the slow cooker

3. Add the tomato paste, parsley, onions, garlic, salt, pepper, basil, and oregano

4. Turn the slow cooker down to LOW and cook for 7 hours

5. Turn the cooker up to HIGH and add the cooked shrimp

6. Cook for another 30 to 45 minutes – until heated through

Makes 8 to 10 servings

Mellow Yellow Chowder

Because Paleolithic eating eliminates regular white potatoes, chowders can take a hit. But, oh, thank goodness for the sweet potato! With a couple of substitutions from traditional chowders, I think you will truly like the change.

Ingredients:

- 1 pound nitrite/nitrate free bacon, cut into pieces (optional)
- 2 large onions, chopped
- 8 celery stalks, sliced
- 5 large sweet potatoes, peeled and cubed
- 4 cups chicken broth
- 2 (13.5 ounce) cans of coconut milk
- 1 (8 ounce) bottle of clam juice (read the label)
- 2 teaspoons kosher or sea salt
- 1 teaspoon coarse black pepper
- 3 bay leaves
- 2 (10 ounce) cans clams, cut into small pieces
- 3 pounds of shrimp, shelled and deveined

Directions:

1. Turn your slow cooker on HIGH so it can warm up while you get your ingredients ready

2. Using a large frying pan, cook the bacon pieces until they are crisp (If you don't use bacon, use 2 tablespoon coconut oil to cook the vegetables)

3. Remove the bacon and drain on a paper towel

4. Remove most of the bacon grease, but leave enough to brown the onions and celery

5. Sauté the onions and celery until soft

6. Place the cooked vegetables in the slow cooker

7. Add the bacon to the cooker

8. Put in the sweet potato cubes

9. Pour in the chicken broth, coconut milk, clam juice, clams, salt, pepper, and bay leaves

10. Turn your slow cooker down to LOW and cook for 5 to 6 hours

11. Turn your slow cooker up to HIGH

12. Take off the lid, remove the bay leaves, and use a potato masher to mash the cooked sweet potatoes.

This will begin to thicken the chowder. Be sure to leave a few little chunks of potato

13. Add the clam pieces and shrimp to the chowder and cook for another hour

Makes 6 to 8 servings

Soups

&

Stews

Hamburger Vegetable Stew

This has been one of my family's favorite stews for a long time. It is easy to fix on the stovetop but also easy to put the ingredients into a slow cooker and let the aromas make you hungry. See what you think.

Ingredients:

- 2 tablespoons coconut oil
- 2 pounds grass-fed ground beef
- 2 onions, chopped
- 4 stalks celery, stalks
- 2 bell pepper – any color – seeded and chopped
- 2 cups fresh mushrooms
- 5 carrots peeled and sliced
- 4 cups fresh green beans, snapped into bite-sized pieces
- 2 (15 ounce) cans sugar free tomato sauce
- 2 quarts organic beef broth
- 1 tablespoon raw honey or pure maple syrup (optional)
- 2 teaspoons celery seed

- 1 tablespoon kosher or sea salt
- 2 teaspoons coarse black pepper

Directions:

1. Turn your slow cooker on HIGH while you get your ingredients ready
2. In a large frying pan, place the coconut oil and let it get hot
3. Place the ground beef into the frying pan and brown completely
4. Now place the browned ground beef into the slow cooker
5. Put the onions, celery, bell peppers, and mushrooms into the frying pan and sauté for 5 minutes
6. Put the sautéed vegetables into the slow cooker
7. Put the carrots, green beans, tomato sauce, beef broth, honey, celery seed, salt and pepper into the slow cooker
8. Stir the ingredients together
9. Cover the cooker and lower the temperature to LOW
10. Cook for 7 to 8 hours

Makes 8 servings

European Beef Stew

This is a recipe I remember making when I got married years ago. It has evolved over time as I have tweaked it to please my family. One final evolution occurred several years ago when I started eating this way. So, here I present a favorite slow cooker recipe – from my family to yours

Ingredients:

- 3 pounds stew meat
- 2 tablespoons arrowroot powder
- ½ teaspoon celery salt
- ¼ teaspoon garlic powder
- ½ teaspoon ground ginger
- ¼ teaspoon pepper
- 5 carrots, peeled and thinly sliced
- 1 (16 ounce) can diced tomatoes, undrained
- ½ cup beef broth
- ¼ cup pure maple syrup or raw honey (optional)
- ¼ cup raisins (optional)

Directions:

1. Turn your slow cooker on HIGH to allow it to heat up while you get your ingredients ready

2. Place the stew beef into the slow cooker

3. In a small bowl, combine the arrowroot powder, celery salt, garlic powder, ground ginger, and pepper

4. Mix thoroughly then sprinkle over the beef

5. Pour the carrots on top of the beef

6. In another bowl, mix the tomatoes in their juice with the broth and pure maple syrup or raw honey

7. Now pour the liquid over the beef

8. Cover the slow cooker and cook on LOW for 7 to 8 hours

9. Add the raisins 30 minutes before serving

Serve over spaghetti squash or mashed cauliflower "potatoes"

Makes 6 to 8 servings

Granny's Butternut Soup

Butternut squash is one of the softer skinned winter squashes so it is easier to cut and peel than several of the other squashes. When the sweetness of the butternut squash meets the tartness of the Granny Smith apples in this soup, it is a great combination.

Ingredients:

- 2 tablespoons coconut oil
- 2 large red onions (for color. You can use any kind you want)
- 6 cups of diced butternut squash – peeled, seeded and cut into cubes
- 4 celery stalks, cut into slices
- 2 large Granny Smith apples, peeled, cored and chopped
- 4 cups natural chicken broth
- 1 tablespoon kosher or sea salt
- 2 teaspoons coarse black pepper
- ¼ teaspoon nutmeg
- ¼ teaspoon cinnamon

- ½ teaspoon cayenne pepper

Directions:

1. Turn your slow cooker on HIGH while you get your ingredients ready

2. On the stovetop, use a large saucepan and melt the coconut oil

3. Place the onions, squash, and celery into the pan and cook until vegetables begin to soften – approximately 10 to 15 minutes.

4. Transfer the vegetables to your slow cooker

5. To the slow cooker, add the chopped apples, chicken broth, salt, pepper, nutmeg, cinnamon, and cayenne pepper

6. Cook on HIGH for 7 to 8 hours and LOW for 10 hours

7. Turn the slow cooker down to WARM if your cooker has this setting; otherwise, LOW

8. Using a stick immerse able blender stick, puree the soup

9. Continue until you have the consistency you desire

10. Taste the soup and adjust the seasonings to your liking

Makes 4 to 6 servings

Kickin' Chicken Vegetable Soup

Chicken soup with vegetables always makes me feel good inside when I eat it, especially on a chilly fall evening. This one will give you some "kick" so beware – your nose may run faster than you! If you have small children, you may want to decrease the spices but I would encourage you to try the full flavor.

Ingredients:

- 2 tablespoons of coconut oil, melted
- 3 - 4 boneless skinless chicken breasts
- 8 cups chicken broth
- 3 garlic cloves, minced
- 2 onions, chopped
- 2 bell peppers, seeded and diced
- 2 zucchini, peeled and diced
- 3 to 4 carrots, peeled and sliced
- 2 cups fresh green beans or frozen
- 2 celery stalks, sliced
- 1 teaspoon dried oregano
- 2 teaspoons chili powder

- 2 teaspoons ground coriander
- 2 teaspoons paprika
- 2 teaspoons ground cumin
- 1 tablespoon kosher or sea salt
- 2 teaspoons coarse black pepper
- 1 cup of your favorite salsa (you decide how hot)

Directions:

1. Turn your slow cooker on HIGH while you get your ingredients ready

2. Put the melted coconut oil on the bottom of your slow cooker or put in the oil and wait for the slow cooker to heat up and melt it

3. Place the chicken breasts into the slow cooker

4. Add all the remaining ingredients to the slow cooker and then stir to mix thoroughly

5. Leave your slow cooker on HIGH if you desire and cook for 8 hours

6. If you wish, you can turn your slow cooker down to LOW and cook for 9 to 10 hours

7. When finished cooking, remove the chicken breasts from the cooker on to a plate and shred the meat

8. Place the shredded meat back into the cooker and mix with the other ingredients

Makes 6 to 8 servings

Sweet Potato Soup

Here is one potato soup that you will really enjoy in your slow cooker. It is great for the holidays or whenever you are in the mood. The syrup and nutmeg give it a hint of pumpkin pie.

Ingredients:

- 2 tablespoons grass-fed butter or coconut oil
- 2 pounds sweet potatoes, peeled and cubed
- 6 cups chicken broth
- 2 onions, chopped
- 2 garlic cloves, minced
- 2 celery stalks, sliced
- 1 medium leek, sliced (use white and pale green parts)
- ½ teaspoon ground cinnamon
- ½ teaspoon ground nutmeg
- 2 tablespoons pure maple syrup (optional)
- 2 cups almond milk, coconut milk or half and half
- ½ cup arrowroot powder

Directions:

1. Turn your slow cooker on to HIGH to heat up while you are getting your ingredients ready

2. Put the butter, potatoes, broth, onions, garlic, celery, leek, cinnamon, nutmeg, and maple syrup into the slow cooker

3. Turn the slow cooker down to LOW and cook for 8 hours

4. About 30 minutes before you want to eat, use a stick blender to puree the soup to the consistency you desire

5. Stir together the milk/half and half together with the arrowroot powder to make a paste without lumps

6. Mix it into the soup and cook 30 more minutes until the soup has thickened and hot throughout

Makes 8 servings

One Pot

Meals

Meaty Chili

I have always enjoyed beans in my chili, but since I have been eating differently and creating my own recipes, I really like it without them. I would much rather fill up on good hearty meat than legumes any day!

Ingredients

- 2 tablespoons coconut oil
- 2 onions, chopped
- 4 pounds grass-fed stew beef (ground beef would be used as well)
- 2 (15 ounce) cans tomato sauce
- 1 (28 ounce) can diced tomatoes
- 2 cups beef stock
- 3 tablespoons chili powder
- 2 teaspoons crushed red peppers
- 2 teaspoons kosher or sea salt
- 1 teaspoon ground cumin

Directions:

1. Turn your slow cooker on HIGH while you get your ingredients ready

2. In a frying pan on your stovetop, place the coconut oil and heat it

3. Sauté the onions until tender

4. Add the stew meat and brown on all sides

5. Transfer the meat and onions to your slow cooker

6. Add the tomato sauce, diced tomatoes, and beef stock and stir together

7. Take a small bowl and mix together the chili powder, red peppers, salt, and cumin

8. Pour combined spices into the slow cooker and gently stir to mix

9. Place the lid on your slow cooker, turn the heat down to LOW and cook for 8 hours (or leave your cooker on HIGH and cook for 4 to 5 – until meat is tender)

Serves 8 to 10 people

Savory Jambalaya

This jambalaya is savory and spicy and is a wonderful comfort food for a chilly fall evening. The nice thing, too, is it is easy to put together and saves a lot of time in the kitchen from other jambalaya recipes I have made in the past. Hope you enjoy this meal as much as I have creating, and eating it!

Ingredients:

- 2 tablespoons coconut oil
- 4 bell peppers - different colors for visual appeal
- 2 onions, chopped
- 2 garlic cloves, minced
- 3 celery stalks, sliced
- 6 cups chicken stock
- 1 (28 ounce) can of organic diced tomatoes, undrained
- 8 ounces of uncooked chicken, diced
- 12 to 16 ounce package of spicy Andouille sausage cut into slices (try to find nitrate/hormone free)
- 2 cups okra (optional)
- 3 tablespoons Cajun Seasoning

- 1/4 cup of your favorite hot sauce (I like Frank's)
- 2 bay leaves
- 2 pounds shrimp – raw, shelled and deveined

Directions:

1. Turn your slow cooker on HIGH while you get your ingredients ready

2. On the stovetop in a skillet, melt the coconut oil

3. When the oil is heated, add the bell peppers, onions, garlic, and celery and sauté until tender

4. Transfer the vegetables to the slow cooker

5. Add the chicken broth, diced tomatoes with the juice, chicken, sausage, okra, Cajun seasoning, hot sauce, and bay leaves

6. Place the lid on your slow cooker and turn the temperature down to LOW

7. Cook for 6 hours

8. About 45 minutes before you want to eat, turn the slow cooker up to HIGH and put in the shrimp

9. Stir to blend the ingredients

10. Replace the cover and cook until the shrimp are fully cooked

11. Serve over cauliflower "rice" or spaghetti squash

Makes 8 to 10 servings

Stuffed Bell Peppers

I remember my mom making these when I was growing up but she always did them in the oven and they were not Paleolithic. Now that I have made them Paleolithic-friendly, they often bring back childhood memories when I am making them. Good stuff – in my head and in my stomach.

Ingredients:

- 2 tablespoons coconut oil
- 2 small onions, finely chopped
- 4 garlic cloves, minced
- 1 celery stalk, finely chopped
- 2 carrots, finely chopped
- 1½ pounds grass-fed ground beef
- 2 cups cooked finely shredded cabbage
- 6 ounces tomato paste
- 1 tablespoon Italian seasonings
- 2 teaspoons kosher or sea salt
- 1 teaspoon coarse black pepper

- 6 bell peppers, colors of your choice, seeded (save the tops)
- ½ cup water or beef broth

Directions:

1. Turn your slow cooker on to HIGH so it can heat up while you get your ingredients ready

2. Using a frying pan on your stovetop, heat up the coconut oil

3. Place the onions, garlic, celery, and carrots in the frying pan and sauté until tender (carrots will still be rather firm)

4. Add the ground beef and brown completely

5. Drain the beef and vegetables

6. In a large bowl, combine the cabbage, tomato paste, Italian seasoning, salt, and pepper and mix thoroughly

7. Take the bell peppers and evenly divide up the ground beef stuffing mix you've just created and place in each pepper

8. Place the filled peppers into your slow cooker and put the tops of the bell peppers back on each one

9. Pour the ½ cup of liquid into the bottom of the slow cooker and put the lid on the cooker

10. Turn your cooker down to LOW and cook for 7 to 8 hours

Makes 6 servings

Beef and Broccoli

I really like Chinese beef and broccoli when I go out, but I'd much rather fix it at home so I know *exactly* what I'm eating. My family and I are very happy with my rendition of this favorite dish so we do not order out much anymore. Did you see how I just saved money?

Ingredients:

- 2 tablespoons coconut oil
- 4 garlic cloves, minced
- 2 onions, chopped
- ½ cup coconut flour or almond flour (more if needed)
- 2 pounds beef, cut in thin strips
- ½ cup coconut aminos
- ¼ cup beef broth
- 4 tablespoons apple cider vinegar
- 2 tablespoons coconut sugar (optional)
- 4 teaspoons sesame oil
- 1 teaspoon crushed red pepper flakes
- 2 bags frozen broccoli florets, thawed
- 2 tablespoons sesame seeds

- 4 cups cooked spaghetti squash or cauliflower rice

Directions:

1. Turn your slow cooker on HIGH while you get your ingredients ready

2. Place the coconut oil in a frying pan on your stovetop and melt over medium heat

3. Sauté the onions and garlic until tender

4. Put into your slow cooker

5. Lightly flour the beef and brown in your frying pan (add a little more coconut oil if necessary)

6. Once browned, transfer the beef to your slow cooker

7. In a bowl, combine the coconut aminos, broth, vinegar, coconut sugar, sesame oil, and pepper flakes and mix together

8. Pour over the beef strips

9. Turn your slow cooker down to LOW and cook for 7 to 8 hours

10. About 1 hour before you are ready to eat, turn your cooker up to HIGH

11. Put in the broccoli, sesame seeds, and squash/rice

12. Stir together and allow to cook for another 45 to 60 minutes

Makes 6 to 8 servings

Sweet Lasagna

I really like lasagna, but when you work hard to avoid pastas and grains, what do you do? Well, in this case, you get creative. I saw on a website where someone had used slices of sweet potatoes in place of noodles and that got me thinking, "Why not do that with my lasagna? With a few tweaks and adjustments, I think you, too, will say, "Awesome!"

If you do not participate in eating dairy products, you will probably want to skip this one, but for those that did participate in eating cheeses once in a while, you will really like this one.

Ingredients:

- 1 pound nitrite/nitrate free bacon, thinly sliced
- 2 onions, chopped
- 3 garlic cloves, minced
- 2 pounds ground beef (lean and grass-fed if possible)
- 4 large sweet potatoes, peeled and thinly sliced (lengthwise for long "noodles" if you wish or cross-cut for easy handling)

- 2 (15 ounce) can Italian-style tomato sauce
- 2 teaspoons dried basil leaves, crumbled
- ½ teaspoon dried oregano
- 1 teaspoon kosher or sea salt
- ½ teaspoon cayenne pepper
- 1 teaspoon paprika
- 1 teaspoon coarse black pepper
- 3 cups aged cheddar, shredded
- 1 cup aged Parmesan cheese, shredded

Directions:

1. Turn your slow cooker on HIGH so it can heat up while you get your ingredients ready

2. In a large frying pan, frying the bacon thoroughly until crispy

3. Remove from the frying pan and drain on a paper towel

4. Pour off the bacon grease

5. Sauté the onions and garlic until onions are tender

6. Put in the ground beef and cook until browned

7. Remove from heat when finished cooking

8. Add the bacon in with the ground beef mixture and combine thoroughly

9. Pour the tomato sauce, basil, oregano, salt, cayenne pepper, paprika and pepper into the ground beef and mix thoroughly

10. In a medium bowl, place the shredded cheddar and shredded Parmesan and mix together

11. Begin by covering the bottom of your slow cooker with a thin layer of ground beef/bacon/sauce mixture

12. Place a layer of "sweet potato noodles" over the beef layer

13. Sprinkle some of the cheddar/Parmesan cheese mixture over the noodles

14. Continue layering in this fashion until your ingredients run out

15. Turn your slow cooker down to LOW and cook for 7 to 8 hours

16. Top off the lasagna with a layer of shredded Parmesan cheese

17. Put the cover back on and allow it to sit for 10 minutes

Makes 6 to 8 servings

Note: Because ricotta and mozzarella cheeses that are normally found in lasagna are not *aged cheeses,* aged Parmesan and cheddar have been used instead.

Side

Dishes

A Note "on the Sides"

In this next section on side dishes, it is fun to have more than one slow cooker going. When you have your main entrée cooking in your 6-quart cooker, you may want to cook a side dish as well. If you have two 6-quart slow cookers like I do, or a smaller 4-quart cooker, you can cook things like sweet potatoes, spaghetti squash, and other dishes at the same time – even desserts if you like.

Check out this section, and if your budget allows or you are having a birthday soon, you might want to get a second, or third slow cooker.

Have fun!

Easy Sweet Potatoes

I really like having a sweet potato now and then but cooking them can leave a sticky mess. To help alleviate this problem, I put a piece of foil inside my slow cooker before I put the potatoes in. Then all I have to do is throw the foil away! See, I told you slow cooking was easy cleanup.

Ingredients:

- ¼ cup of water
- Number of sweet potatoes for your family

Directions:

1. Pour the water into the bottom of the slow cooker

2. Line your slow cooker with foil so it goes part-way up the sides of the cooker

3. Turn your slow cooker on HIGH so it can warm up while you are getting your potatoes ready

4. Wash the outside of the potatoes with water

5. Place each potato inside the slow cooker

6. Put the lid on and put the temperature on LOW

7. Cook for 7 to 8 hours

Slow Cooker Spaghetti Squash

Since turning "Paleo," I eat a lot more spaghetti squash than I used to. Because I use it a lot as part of a main meal where pasta noodles are called for. It is so nice to cook it in the slow cooker. Now when my main dish is done, so is my "pasta."

Note: Early in the season, spaghetti squash has a thinner shell than when it is later in the season. The skin becomes thicker as the season progresses so you may need to cook it a little longer on occasion. Just experiment as I do.

Ingredients:

- 1 spaghetti squash

Directions:

1. Turn your slow cooker on HIGH while you get the squash ready

2. Rinse the outside of the squash thoroughly with water

3. Place the squash inside your slow cooker

4. Leave the slow cooker on HIGH and cook for 4 hours or turn it down to LOW and cook for 7 to 8 hours

Squashed Apples

This dish is almost good enough to call a dessert. In fact, feel free to use it as one.

Ingredients:

- 4 pounds butternut squash, peeled and cubed (about 8 cups)
- 5 sweet apples (like Galas), peeled and cut into slices
- 4 tablespoons grass-fed butter, melted
- 1 cup coconut sugar (measures like real sugar - optional)
- 3 tablespoons arrowroot powder
- 1 teaspoon ground cinnamon
- ½ teaspoon ginger
- ¼ teaspoon nutmeg
- ⅛ teaspoon cardamom
- ½ cup chopped nuts (your choice)
- ½ cup raisins

Directions:

1. Turn your slow cooker on HIGH so it can warm up while you get your ingredients ready

2. Place half of the squash cubes into the bottom of your slow cooker

3. Put half of the apple slices on top of the squash

4. In a bowl, mix the melted butter, sugar, arrowroot powder, cinnamon, ginger, nutmeg, and cardamom and blend thoroughly

5. Pour half this mixture over the apples and squash

6. Repeat the layering one more time

7. Lower your slow cooker to LOW and cook for 7 hours or leave on HIGH and cook for 4 hours

8. Top with nuts and raisins before serving

Serves 6 to 8 people

Note: You could also use sweet potatoes in place of butternut squash if desired

Mashed Cauliflower

Cauliflower is a vegetable that is eaten a great deal around our house. Whether it is raw with a dip or steamed with broccoli, I am always experimenting. Here is a side dish of cauliflower I think you will enjoy, plus it cooks right along with any main dish in another slow cooker.

Ingredients:

- 1 large head of cauliflower
- 3 cups of chicken broth
- 3 garlic cloves, minced
- 1 teaspoon onion powder
- ½ teaspoon kosher or sea salt
- ½ teaspoon pepper
- 2 tablespoons grass-fed butter
- 2 tablespoons chives

Directions:

1. Turn your slow cooker on HIGH while you get your ingredients ready

2. Wash and break the cauliflower head into pieces and place in the cooker

3. Add the broth, garlic, onion powder, salt, and pepper to the cooker

4. Place the lid on the cooker and continue to cook on HIGH for 3 hours or turn the cooker down to LOW for 6 hours

5. Carefully pour off as much broth as you can

6. Using a stick blender, process the cauliflower until you get the texture and consistency you desire

7. Top with chives

Makes 6 servings

Grown-up Spicy Carrots

This side dish is very easy to put together and offers some wonderful flavors to any main dish. Try it and see what you think.

Ingredients:

- ½ pound nitrate/nitrite free bacon cut into small pieces
- 2 tablespoons coconut oil
- 2 onions, chopped
- 4 garlic cloves, minced
- 3 pounds carrots, sliced
- ⅓ cup spicy mustard
- ⅓ cup raw honey or pure maple syrup (I would definitely use this ingredient)
- 2 tablespoons balsamic vinegar
- ⅛ cup chicken broth
- 1 teaspoon ground ginger
- ¼ teaspoon cayenne pepper
- 1 teaspoon salt

Directions:

1. Turn your slow cooker on HIGH so it can warm up while you get your ingredients ready

2. In a frying pan on your stovetop, cook the bacon until done

3. Drain on a paper towel

4. Drain the grease, but leave a little to sauté the onions and garlic. Cook until tender

5. Place the carrots on the bottom of the slow cooker

6. Transfer the onions and garlic from the frying pan to the cooker

7. Sprinkle the bacon pieces on top

8. In a bowl, combine the mustard, honey, vinegar, broth, ginger, pepper, and salt and mix thoroughly

9. Pour the liquid gently over the carrots

10. Place the lid on the cooker and lower the temperature to LOW

11. Cook for 7 hours

Makes 6 to 8 servings

Quick Breads & Muffins

A Quick Note about Breads

Yes, I know that quick breads are not usually cooked in a slow cooker, but you can if you do not want a hot kitchen and you know a few tricks.

I do not know about you, but sometimes I still want a good piece of bread or muffin with my cup of coffee or with my soup.

This next section includes numerous recipes that have become some of my favorites and can be cooked in your slow cooker in a bread loaf pan. **Please note: you will need to use a 6-quart oblong slow cooker in order to fit most bread pans inside.**

In the recipes that follow, most have some type of sweetener in them. They are mainly raw honey, pure maple syrup, or coconut sugar. Sweeteners are optional, but eliminating them will change the texture slightly. *You will just have to decide if you want the little bit added in or it.* If you are like me, you seldom even eat muffins or breads, so when you do, it falls well within

Mark Sisson's 80/20 rule (eat Paleolithic 80% of the time and have a little fun the other 20%).

Before you do so, I want to walk you through the process so you will know how to do this. Once you learn it, you can make just about any muffin or sweet bread recipe you want.

1. Because regular muffin pans will not fit inside a slow cooker, you will have to cook these recipes in a loaf pan that fits inside your slow cooker. **Be sure to test to see if your loaf pan fits inside your slow cooker before you start!** Most 6-quart oblong slow cookers will hold a regular bread pan (8½ x 4½).

2. You will want to form four small balls made out of foil to elevate your loaf pan off the bottom of your slow cooker. If you have a small rack that fits in the bottom of your slow cooker, you can use that instead.

3. Be sure to spray your pan with coconut oil spray or grease it with coconut oil. Coconut oil can withstand high temperatures and will not burn.

4. Once you treat your bread pan, place it down into the slow cooker, on top of the foil balls, and turn the slow cooker on and up to HIGH. This will allow it to preheat – just as you do your oven. If you wish, you can place your loaf pan down into the slow cooker, onto the foil balls, before you fill with the batter or wait until the pan

is filled. Be sure to use hand protection if you wait until after it is filled so you do not get burned by the sides of the slow cooker.

5. While each slow cooker is different, it will take about 2 hours for your loaf to cook completely. Test the center for doneness using a toothpick or cake tester.

6. When cooking these recipes, **be sure you turn the lid slightly crooked so steam can escape,** or prop your lid open with a couple of toothpicks. You do not want the condensation that normally forms on the lid to fall into your loaf.

7. Once your loaf is thoroughly cooked, allow it to sit in the pan for 15 minutes, and then carefully dump it out onto a cooling rack.

8. Once it is thoroughly cooled, which takes about another 30 minutes to an hour, you can slice yourself a

piece and feast on the flavor. (Can you tell I like nuts?) And by the way, grass-fed butter is optional.

Let this be the start of some wonderful baking at your house as you experiment and try new Paleolithic breads in your slow cooker!

So, without any further adieu, I present to you ***Paleolithic-style quick breads and muffins!***

Banana Bread

Ingredients:

- 6 eggs
- ⅓ cup raw honey
- ⅓ cup coconut oil
- 2 ripe bananas
- 1 tablespoon pure vanilla extract
- ½ cup coconut flour
- 1 teaspoon baking soda
- ½ teaspoon salt
- 1 cup of your favorite nuts, chopped (optional)

Directions:

1. Turn your slow cooker on HIGH while you prepare your bread recipe and place a rack or 4 small foil balls in the bottom of your cooker

2. In a blender, place the eggs, honey, coconut oil, bananas, and vanilla

3. Blend until all ingredients are thoroughly mixed

4. In a medium bowl, thoroughly combine the flour, baking soda, salt and nuts

5. Pour the banana mixture into the dry ingredients and stir until dry ingredients are wet

6. Generously grease your loaf pan

7. Pour the batter into the pan and place the pan inside the cooker

8. Prop the lid open slightly so condensation can escape

9. Cook on HIGH for at least 2 hours

10. Test for doneness and cook longer if necessary

11. When finished cooking, remove from the cooker and allow to set for about 15 minutes

12. Gently dump the bread on to a cooling rack

13. Cut when ready!

If you want to make muffins instead, you will have to use your oven.

1. Preheat oven to 350 degrees

2. Follow the instructions as stated above, but pour the batter into greased muffin tins

3. Bake 20-25 minutes

Makes 12 muffins

Pumpkin Bread

Ingredients:

- 6 eggs
- ⅓ cup raw honey
- ⅓ cup coconut oil
- 2 ripe bananas
- ½ cup canned pumpkin
- 1 teaspoon pure vanilla extract
- ¾ cup coconut flour
- 1 teaspoon baking soda
- ½ teaspoon salt
- 1 teaspoon ground cinnamon
- ½ teaspoon ground nutmeg
- ⅛ teaspoon ground ginger
- 1 cup of your favorite nuts, chopped (optional)

Directions:

1. Turn your slow cooker on HIGH while you prepare your bread recipe and place a rack or 4 small foil balls in the bottom of your cooker

2. In a blender, place the eggs, honey, coconut oil, bananas, pumpkin, and vanilla

3. Blend until all ingredients are thoroughly mixed

4. In a medium bowl, thoroughly combine the flour, baking soda, salt, cinnamon, nutmeg, ginger and nuts

5. Pour the wet mixture into the dry ingredients and stir until dry ingredients are wet

6. Generously grease your loaf pan

7. Pour the batter into the pan and place the pan inside the cooker

8. Prop the lid open slightly so condensation can escape

9. Cook on HIGH for at least 2 hours

10. Test for doneness and cook longer if necessary

11. When finished cooking, remove from the cooker and allow to set for about 15 minutes

12. Gently dump the bread on to a cooling rack

13. Cut when ready!

If you want to make muffins instead, you will have to use your oven.

1. Preheat oven to 350 degrees

2. Follow the instructions as stated above, but pour the batter into greased muffin tins

3. Bake 25–30 minutes

Makes 12 to 15 muffins

Cranberry Bread

Ingredients:

- 6 eggs (room temperature)
- 1/3 cup raw honey
- 4 tablespoons butter
- 2 teaspoons pure vanilla extract
- 1/2 cup coconut flour
- 1/2 teaspoon sea salt
- 1/2 teaspoon baking powder
- 1½ teaspoons cinnamon
- 1 cup cranberries, thawed if frozen

Directions:

1. Turn on your slow cooker to HIGH while you get your ingredients ready

2. Spray or apply coconut oil to the sides and bottom of your loaf pan

3. In a blender, put the eggs, honey, butter, and vanilla

4. Allow the blender to run on low or medium while you mix up the dry ingredients in a bowl

5. Add the wet ingredients into the dry ingredients and mix thoroughly

6. Stir in the cranberries

7. Pour the batter into the loaf pan

8. Place the lid on your slow cooker, using a couple of toothpicks to prop it up to reduce any condensation

9. Cook on HIGH for 2 hours

10. Using a toothpick, check for doneness

11. Remove from the slow cooker and place the pan on a cooling rack for 15 minutes

12. Using a knife, scrape the sides loose and gently invert the bread pan so the loaf is on the cooling rack

13. Allow to cool completely

14. Slice and butter if desired

Butter Bread

Ingredients:

- 8 large eggs (room temperature)
- 1 stick butter
- ¼ cup raw honey
- 2/3 cup coconut flour
- ½ teaspoon baking powder
- ¾ teaspoon sea salt

Directions:

1. Turn on your slow cooker to HIGH while you get your ingredients ready

2. Spray or apply coconut oil to the sides and bottom of your loaf pan

3. In a blender, put the eggs and turn the blender on HIGH for 2 minutes

4. Now add the butter and honey

5. Allow the blender to run on low or medium while you mix up the dry ingredients in a bowl

6. Add the wet ingredients into the dry ingredients and mix thoroughly

7. Pour the batter into the loaf pan

8. Place the lid on your slow cooker, using a couple of toothpicks to prop it up to reduce any condensation

9. Cook on HIGH for 2 hours

10. Using a toothpick, check for doneness

11. Remove from the slow cooker and place the pan on a cooling rack for 15 minutes

12. Using a knife, scrape the sides loose and gently invert the bread pan so the loaf is on the cooling rack

13. Allow to cool completely

14. Slice and butter if desired

Blueberry Coconut Bread

Ingredients:

- 3 large eggs (room temperature)
- ½ cup unsweetened applesauce
- ½ cup raw honey
- ½ cup almond butter
- 1 cup almond flour
- ½ teaspoon baking powder
- ½ teaspoon baking soda
- ½ teaspoon ground cinnamon
- ½ teaspoon sea salt
- ¾ cup shredded coconut (unsweetened)
- 1 cup fresh blueberries (thawed if frozen)

Directions:

1. Turn on your slow cooker to HIGH while you get your ingredients ready

2. Spray or apply coconut oil to the sides and bottom of your loaf pan

3. In a blender, put the eggs, applesauce, honey, and almond butter

4. Allow the blender to run on low or medium while you mix up the dry ingredients in a bowl

5. Add the wet ingredients into the dry ingredients and mix thoroughly

6. Stir in the shredded coconut and blueberries

7. Pour the batter into the loaf pan

8. Place the lid on your slow cooker, using a couple of toothpicks to prop it up to reduce any condensation

9. Cook on HIGH for 2 hours

10. Using a toothpick, check for doneness

11. Remove from the slow cooker and place the pan on a cooling rack for 15 minutes

12. Using a knife, scrape the sides loose and gently invert the bread pan so the loaf is on the cooling rack

13. Allow to cool completely

14. Slice and butter if desired

15. Serve hot.

Beverages

Before You Take a Drink

Those of us who practice living a Paleolithic lifestyle know that fruit drinks are not the norm. However, if you allow yourself to live by the 80/20 rule like Mark Sisson does and many of my other Paleolithic buddies do, (meaning you "behave" yourself 80% of the time and allow indulgences the other 20%), on occasion it is okay to splurge and have some cider once in a while.

Holiday time is a great time of year to offer a spiced cider drink to friends and family, and it makes the house smell fabulous.

So, if you allow yourself an occasional sip of cider, then enjoy these recipes.

Here's to your health!

Spiced Apple Tea

Ingredients:

- 1 gallon of fresh apple cider
- 3 Granny Smith apples, peeled and thinly sliced
- 6 cinnamon sticks
- 8 whole cloves
- 8 herbal tea bags, any flavor

Directions:

1. Turn your slow cooker on HIGH while you get your ingredients ready

2. Pour the apple cider into the slow cooker

3. Place the apple slices, cinnamon sticks, cloves and tea bags down into the cider

4. Allow the cooker to remain on HIGH and cook for 3 hours

5. Take out the floating objects or scoop out what you want to drink and allow objects to remain as they continue to flavor the cider

Makes one gallon

Cider with a Twist

Ingredients:

- 1 gallon fresh apple cider
- 1 cup unsweetened cranberry juice
- 2 navel oranges, washed, unpeeled, and sliced
- 10 whole cloves
- 4 cinnamon sticks
- 10 whole allspice
- 2 cups coconut sugar or raw honey
- 1 teaspoon ground cinnamon

Directions:

1. Turn on your slow cooker to HIGH while you get your ingredients ready

2. Pour the apple cider and cranberry juice into the slow cooker

3. Place the orange slices into the cider

4. If desired you can use a small piece of cheesecloth or a cheesecloth bag to put the remaining ingredients into and tie with a twist tie

5. Leave the slow cooker on HIGH and cook for 4 hours or turn the cooker down to LOW and allow the smells to fill the house for 7 to 8 hours

6. Remove the cheesecloth or tea ball and scoop cider into mugs

Makes one gallon

Slow Brewing Wassail

Ingredients:

- 1 gallon fresh apple cider
- 2 cups unsweetened cranberry juice
- 7 naval oranges, 6 of them squeezed, 1 studded with whole cloves
- 10 cinnamon sticks
- 15 whole allspice
- 1 cup coconut sugar or raw honey

Directions:

1. Turn your slow cooker on HIGH while you get your ingredients ready

2. Pour the apple cider and the cranberry juice into the slow cooker

3. Pour the fresh orange juice into the slow cooker

4. Stir to blend the juices

5. Place the orange studded with whole cloves into the cooker

6. Place the cinnamon sticks, allspice, and sugar into a cheesecloth bag and put it down into the cider mixture

7. Leave your cooker on HIGH and cook for 4 hours or lower the cooker to LOW and cook for 7 hours while you enjoy the wonderful smells

8. Remove the cheesecloth bag

9. Serve and enjoy

Makes one gallon

About the Author

Amelia Simons is a food enthusiast, wife, and mother of five. Frustrated with traditional dieting advice, she stumbled upon the Paleolithic lifestyle of eating and has never looked back. Without bothering to count calories or stress about endless hours of exercise, eating the Paleolithic way enabled Amelia and her husband to effortlessly drop pounds and lower their cholesterol.

Amelia now enjoys sharing the Paleolithic philosophy with friends and readers and finding new ways to turn favorite recipes into healthy alternatives.

Additional Resources

Be sure to check out my other resources.

Complete Paleo Meals: A Paleo Cookbook Featuring Paleo Comfort Foods

Gluten-Free Slow Cooker: Easy Recipes for a Gluten Free Diet

Paleolithic Slow Cooker Soups and Stews: Healthy Family Gluten-Free Recipes

Going Paleolithic: A Quick Start Guide for a Gluten-Free Diet

4 Weeks of Fabulous Paleolithic Breakfasts

4 MORE Weeks of Fabulous Paleolithic Breakfasts

4 Weeks of Fabulous Paleolithic Lunches

4 Weeks of Fabulous Paleolithic Dinners

The Ultimate Paleolithic Collection

Acknowledgements

Many thanks to the following photographers from *Flickr.com*:

- Janine
- Iain Farrell
- The Happy Cynic
- BBQ Junkie
- stu_spivack
- David Kracht

Made in the USA
Lexington, KY
22 June 2014